A Love Affair with Landscape

Poems

by

Jay Appleton

The Wildhern Press 2009

Published by

The Wildhern Press

131 High St.
Teddington
Middlesex TW11 8HH

www.echo-library.com

ISBN 978-1-84830-098-9

IN MEMORIAM

IRIS APPLETON
(1921 - 2006)

The love of landscape was a sort of twine
That bound your vision of the world to mine

Front cover
Iris Appleton on the Malvern Hills, Worcestershire

I have to acknowledge with gratitude
the help and support of many friends
in particular
Gwen and Norman Staveley.

Contents

PROLOGUE

There is a sense in which we are all bilingual. The two languages we speak we can call, for want of better words, 'prosaic' and 'poetic'. They look deceptively similar. They employ the same words, the same phrases, the same sentence-construction, often the same grammar and syntax, but the rules governing their use are significantly different. If you are a physicist, a lawyer or a historian a single *non-sequitur,* (a sentence in which the conclusion does **not follow** from the premise), is enough to destroy your argument, even, perhaps, your reputation. If you are a poet you may string together as many as you like and get away with it.

Having spent my professional life as an academic geographer I have always had to be careful to comply with the rules of the prosaic mode and to be suspicious of allowing the poetic to intrude and prejudice the academic validity of what I had to say. As a lover of landscape I was deeply aware that, if reason ruled, emotion was always knocking at the door and had to be viewed with great suspicion. On retirement I was no longer shackled by the same fetters, and, just so long as I did not claim that my poetic expressions carried the same sort of authority as what Richard Dawkins would call 'evidence-based' reasoning, I was free to go where I liked down this other path of exploration.

In fact my freedom was not complete, because I exchanged one set of shackles for another, the rules of scientific logic for the rules of prosody, which Chambers Twentieth Century Dictionary defines as 'the study of versification' and which, in turn, generally means metrical (often rhyming) verse. I did not *have* to submit to this other tyranny; it is my choice. Much, perhaps most, of the poetry being written today has dispensed with metre and rhyme, but for some of us 'verse' devoid of either is lacking components which, until a hundred and fifty years ago, were assumed to be a defining part of poetry, and we cling tenaciously to the right to use them still if we choose.

Now that I have exchanged one tyrannical mistress for another, without renouncing loyalty to either, I have put together this little collection of poems with a view to inviting you to explore with me some of those areas which I have already visited in my academic pursuits, but this time following paths which were then regarded as out of bounds. Emancipation, therefore, has been only partial, but perhaps, if we put these two modes of exploration together, the prosaic and the poetic, and provided we do not confuse their complementary roles, we may somewhat enrich our general experience of 'landscape', which for practical purposes I will define as 'the environment visually perceived'.

ABERLOGIE BAY

I've just returned from Aberlogie Bay
Full of re-kindled images of you,
Re-visiting those places on the way
Where we would stop to revel in the view.
I felt your presence on that stony track
Under the cliff and past the waterfall.
I struggled on to Marston Woods and back,
Which, if you hear me now, you must recall.
I've come to tell you, like I always do,
What I've been up to, where I've been and why,
And, even if I can't get through to you,
I can imagine how you would reply.
By such conceits I wishfully contrive
To keep a little bit of you alive.

AEROCARTOGRAPHY

I'd like to meet the enterprising chap
Who understands my curiosity
And furnishes the aircraft with a map
Plotting our progress over land and sea.
Most passengers ignore geography.
Provided they can reach their journey's end
They tend to treat the route with apathy;
The detail simply drives them round the bend.
But there's a story written on the ground,
And we who try to read it from the sky,
In Bunyan's phrase, do but ourselves confound
Without a reference to fix it by.
So, nameless friend, whoever you may be,
Thank you for giving back my sanity.

AKENBURY HEAD

At Auntie Katy's I could lie in bed
And watch the light on Akenbury Head.
The intermittent flashing of the light
Challenged the inky blackness of the night,
And I was able, twenty miles away,
To get the sense of what it had to say:
'Take heed, ye mariners who sail the sea,
'Night is the proper time for tragedy!'
But little boys, tucked safely up in bed,
Are not in peril from the sea; instead
The visual telegraph is freed to deal
With all the great anxieties they feel.
No childish need could ever come above
Assurance of secure parental love.
So Akenbury in the midnight sky
Became a substitute paternal eye,
Or, in that state of cosy drowsiness,
The symbol of a motherly caress.
Although the light repeatedly went out
Its re-appearance never was in doubt.
Often, when I had tried to find a way
To solve the various problems of the day,
I'd struggled hard enough, but in the end
Had to consult my Akenbury friend.
Then, when the alien world of womanhood
Showed promise of some unexpected good
A lighthouse seemed a safer place to start
Exploring the commitments of the heart
Than risking a disastrous love affair

With some inconstant girl who didn't care.
What my imagination could invest
With amorous significance was best,
And with the help of Akenbury Light
My lover flashed her secrets through the night.
I knew there was no organising sense,
No thinking, rational intelligence
To operate the Akenbury Light,
No brain behind those signals in the night,
Nor did it ever cross my trusting mind
That it could be malicious or unkind,
But night by night it was my joy to spend
An hour communicating with my friend.
Now times have changed, and sadly in the night
Radio-beacons have replaced the light,
And little boys who look for it in vain
Must snuggle underneath the counterpane
And search within a warm and comfy bed
To find the ghost of Akenbury Head.
With luck the lighthouse and its magic beam
Will be resuscitated in a dream.

AMERICAN HERITAGE

Americans, in my experience,
Are seldom lacking in self-confidence,
And yet the founding fathers, it appears,
Back in those early nation-building years,
Displayed one sign of insecurity:
They lacked the mark of authenticity.
At last the settlers hit upon a cure:
They simply stole the old nomenclature,
Borrowing names without apology
Which graced the cities of antiquity.
They'd build a modest, unpretentious home
And find the arrogance to call it Rome.
New upstart towns competed to abuse
Old names like Athens, Troy and Syracuse.
In Athens, thanks to this phenomenon,
You'll search in vain to find the Parthenon,
And never mind where Memphis used to be,
Most people think it's now in Tennessee.
But cultural respectability
Doesn't require a phoney pedigree,
Nor can a reputation ever be
Supported by a bogus ancestry.
To some philosophers the thought occurred
This situation simply was absurd,
And, keen to put an end to their distress,
They found their answer in the wilderness.
The forests which sporadically spanned
The bosom of their new-discovered land
Were worthy symbols of antiquity,
Older than anything in Italy.

9

Sequoias, still alive in Oregon,
Were saplings in the days of Solomon.
The Hudson River still appeared to flow
Much as it did ten thousand years ago.
The Catskill Mountains flourished long before
The time of Homer and the Trojan War.
Surely they had the majesty, the age
To represent the nation's heritage!
Nothing in Latium or Attica
Could match the thunder of Niagara!
New York just wasn't old enough to be
A fitting symbol of antiquity.
The Woolworth Building and the Guggenheim
Are products of a very recent time,
Nor are there many buildings in the West
To rouse an antiquarian's interest.
That work of art that spans the Golden Gate,
Though beautiful, came relatively late.
Having no ruins from antiquity
No temples of a pagan deity,
People began to consecrate their own,
Beginning with the awesome Yellowstone.
Authorities were quick to designate
National Parks in many a rustic state.
Outdoor cathedrals in this present age
Now dominate the country's heritage.
The culture that we leave behind is what
We add to assets we've already got,
Chief among which, by popular consent,
Must be the natural environment.

THE ANIMISTIC MYTH

In primitive communities you'll find
The simple unsophisticated mind
Investing all the rivers, all the trees
With animistic personalities.
Through education we have left behind
Images of this elemental kind;
Our modem understanding is at odds
With woodland deities and river-gods.
So why, I wonder, when my roving eye
Falls on a mountain, soaring in the sky,
Do I invariably seem to see
A watchful sentinel protecting me?
I must admit to see a mountain thus
Is rationally quite ridiculous,
Yet in a very realistic sense
It is an every-day experience,
A fallacy the probing intellect
Seems totally unable to reject.
Of course it's pretty obvious to me
A mountain never *is* a deity;
You'll never catch me dropping on my knees
In veneration of the Pyrenees
Or sacrificing to Mount Ararat;
Nothing as crudely primitive as that;
And yet I feel a certain reverence
For every awe-inspiring eminence.
Whether or not they claim divinity

I find in them a personality.
The hills and mountains of my native land
Will serve to illustrate the case in hand.
Ben Nevis is a gross, lethargic heap
Incapable of anything but sleep,
Unlike the Cuillin in the Isle of Skye
Whose naked needles pierce the searching eye.
Those great escarpments like the Millstone Grit,
Huge couchant beasts, unsleeping as they sit
In contemplation of the vale below,
Observe us mortals passing to and fro.
The Brecon Beacons and the Wolds, you'll find,
Would also represent this 'watchdog' kind.
I get the feeling unmistakably
They've nothing else to do but shelter me.
The water-deities? It's time they went,
Drowned in the torrent of enlightenment.
The woodland gods have also ceased to be,
Felled by the chain-saw of modernity,
So now it's just the mountains that survive
To keep the animistic myth alive.

AULD REEKIE

Here was their geologic heritage,
A land of rocks and vulcanicity.
Here, in a turbulent and lawless age,
They built a haven of security.
Succeeding generations grafted on
A masterplan of Georgian symmetry,
Giving the Scots a new criterion
Of style and classical urbanity.
From Edinburgh Castle's battlements
Across the silvered waters of the Forth,
A panoramic spectacle presents
The metamorphic mountains of the North.
Out of the tangled threads of history
Auld Reekie weaves her complex tapestry.

THE BOOMING BELL OF BUILDWAS

The somnolent Sabrina   *(R.Severn)*
  Flows from her native Wales
And stealthily meanders
  Through Shropshire's sleepy vales,
Until at Buildwas Abbey
  She hears a phantom bell
Which seems to say 'Sabrina,
  'Farewell, my friend, farewell!'

From Criggion and The Breidden
  To Broseley and to Hay,
By cottage, farm and steeple
  She loops her lazy way,
Then, bursting through the defile,
  Emancipated, freed,
She hears the bell of Buildwas,
  'God speed, my friend, God speed!'

The folk who in that country
  Pursued their rustic ways
Completed in contentment
  The cycle of their days,
As each one passed the portal
  In hope of pastures new,
The funeral bell kept tolling
  'Adieu, my friend, adieu!'

I too have felt the heartache
  Of that nostalgic land.
The painful pangs of parting
  I too can understand.
I watch the daylight draining
  Out of the western sky
And hear the bell intoning
  'Good-bye, my friend, good-bye!'

CAPITULATION

It's round about this time of day,
I've done the things I have to do,
And as the landscape fades away
I settle down to think of you.

I sit and think of you and me
Here in the fading of the light,
Watching the day submissively
Capitulating to the night.

Didn't we too capitulate,
Obedient to our destiny,
Submitting to our welcome fate?
We did, my darling, didn't we?

But destiny's a cruel thing,
And when she calls for sacrifice,
Destiny brooks no bargaining;
Capitulation is the price.

Too feeble then to raise your voice
Defiantly to challenge fate,
Sadly, my dear, you had no choice
But meekly to capitulate.

So here I sit revisiting
The day you bravely lost the fight,
Remembering, remembering,
As day capitulates to night.

THE CHESTERFIELD CANAL

When trumpets heralded my birth
And bursting belfries pealed,
Then was I cradled in the earth
Of cosy Chesterfield.

Once, where my placid waters wind
The busy boatmen went;
A crooked spire they left behind
To seek a crooked Trent.

The clatter of the horses' shoes
I listen for in vain;
The longboats with their homely crews
Will never pass again.

If human aspirations fly
Towards a life to be,
Why should the water-gods deny
Me immortality?

Mourn not the glorious past, but keep
Your tryst with me tonight.
The more the lazy boatmen sleep
The more the fish will bite!

CLOUDSPOTTING

The cosy cloister of my bungalow
Provides a harbour out of which to go
Beyond the reach of such intrepid men
As Shackleton and Scott and Amundsen.
Here from my chair I watch the winter scene
Reflected in the television screen,
Vicariously entering a space
Not habitable by the human race.
The cold components of the winter sky
Awaken my imaginative eye
To change the threatening clouds of snow and ice
Into an orogenic paradise.
The towering pinnacles of cumulus,
Protean, mutable and nebulous,
Have now become quite solid once again
And formed themselves into a mountain chain.
Here, from a sheltered vantage-point below,
I calculate the way one has to go.
By circumventing every precipice
And giving dodgy surfaces a miss
One overcomes each obstacle and hence
Attains the summit of this eminence.
I recommend this practice as a sort
Of substitution for a winter sport;
There is no risk of suffering a fall
Or any dire catastrophe at all,
No need to fear the airless stratosphere;

18

We've charged with oxygen the upper air,
Slowed down the raging jetstream up on high
And breathed new warmth into the winter sky.
As long as I can use my cloistered eyes
To roam among those cloud-embellished skies,
What right have I to moan about my fate
With undiscovered worlds to penetrate?

THE CONSECRATION OF STOCKPORT VIADUCT

Is it a temple of some merchant muse?
A monument to some commercial cult?
A cloister of some sordid soulless sect?
This symmetry of looping, leaping arcs,
Cast in a mould of rounded Roman shapes,
Dissects the sky, whose ailing winter light
Strikes at its roots and dies in the attempt.
Out of the hollow belly of the north
Glides unannounced a jointed caravan
With serpentine and fleeting fluency,
And with a squeal that rips the clammy air
It seems to skim the misty parapet.
The light-suspended body-fabric creaks
And gently heaves and quickens on the rail
While underneath the beetling bogies spin
And hum and drum and click across the clints.
Remote and mute and dyed in yellow light
A lone community that comes and goes
Creeps through the sky anonymous. And when
The syncopation of the wheels is dead,
And when the wake of swirling steam is healed
The stilted frame still pecks a loping line
Across the valley to perpetuate
The transient image. Let the priest pronounce,
Though the gaunt ghost of Ruskin break his heart,
The pagan colonnade is sanctified.

DEFLECTED VISTA

The thing I like about an avenue
Is how it takes possession of the eye,
Steers it directly where it's going to -
That faraway, magnetic patch of sky.
But if that vistal corridor is bent,
Thus cutting short the visibility,
It doesn't seem to put us off the scent;
It merely feeds our curiosity.
We humans daily struggle to survive.
By instinct we are programmed to explore;
It's part of how we keep ourselves alive.
That is what curiosity is for!
Deflected vistas therefore serve to show
How overwhelming is the urge to know.

DREAMSCAPE

Landscape is such an all-embracing thing.
It covers land, it covers sea and sky.
We can define it as encompassing
The world as apprehended by the eye.

But, as we go about our daily lives,
Making a map of what we gaze upon,
Only a little part of it survives,
The rest is destined for oblivion.

So, when our waking selves are safe in bed,
Our sleeping selves are very soon at play,
Ferreting through those scrap-heaps in the head
To re-deploy what's left of yesterday.

Out of our semi-conscious memory
We build a semi-replicated scene
Bringing to life a new reality,
A kind of parody of what has been.

The people we encounter in a dream
Retain their several identities,
Yet they are never quite the folk they seem;
They've always changed their personalities.

Likewise the places where we work and play
Present a new and unfamiliar sight.
Cities and towns, familiar in the day,
Look different in the middle of the night.

When what we dream replaces what we see
Accurate images are left behind,
We lose the landscapes of reality
And substitute the landscapes of the mind.

I had a vivid dream the other day.
Driving from Liverpool to Manchester,
I crossed a range of mountains on the way
Which common knowledge tells me isn't there.

I longed to find those mountains once again.
And see the view that set my heart on fire,
That bird's-eye panorama of the plain,
My reconstructed map of Lancashire.

Why is it, then, I always seem to find,
Comparing dreams with actuality,
Those dreamscapes processed in the dormant mind
More charismatic than reality?

EVENSONG

When evening patterns out a tree
And willows hang from fading skies,
Perception then in distance lies
And nearness brings obscurity.

The skyscape, of her sun bereaved,
Carves out more clear the mountain-sides,
While the herbaceous border hides
A thousand secrets unperceived.

The noises falling on the ear
Slip softly in from far away;
In faint harmonics they convey
Echoes of things no longer near.

The sports-car, whining up the hill,
The late guffaws of village boys,
Reduced to miniatures of noise,
Ruffle the silence and are still.

Against the fainting afterglow
A tattered bat in hairpin flight
Salutes the entry of the night
With crisply quivering shadow-show.

Fit out the eyes with evening wings,
For, when the source of light declines
And only in the distance shines,
What sense is left in nearer things?

GREEN SKY AT NIGHT

The winter sky is blue but bitter cold,
A not infrequent January scene,
And as the sunset turns it into gold
There comes a momentary tinge of green.
The brightening yellow of the setting sun
Pushes aside the swiftly fading blue,
And, once the merging process has begun,
A green component joins the other two.
Perhaps some jealous verdant deity,
Aspires to dominate the winter sky,
Anxious to seize an opportunity
Which blue and gold successfully deny.
A moment's glimpse of green is all that we
Are charitably privileged to see.

HANDEL AND THE BRIGHTON LINE

Riding one morning on the Brighton train,
I left the great metropolis behind,
Happy to see the rural scene again,
Long out of sight but seldom out of mind.
Something about that Wealden countryside
Awakens half-forgotten memories;
Arcadian yearnings soon are satisfied
By woods and fields and cosy cottages.
At last we reach the Chalk escarpment, where
A tunnel takes us under Clayton Down,
From which, emerging in the open air,
We find ourselves already in the town.
From Eastbourne on the left swings into sight
A branch about to join its trunk again.
The Worthing line, approaching from the right,
Describes a tangent underneath the train.
The clutter of the terminal approach,
A signal box, the creaking on the bend,
The bogies squealing underneath the coach,
Announce the imminence of Journey's End.
Though Handel never saw a railway train
Or understood a railwayman's designs,
His music tells us time and time again
He was no stranger to converging lines.
Think how he took those narratives of old,
Abstracted from the Hebrew Testament,
Or else those tales the Greeks and Romans told,
Leading us through Arcadia as he went.
Out of the distance comes a melody,

Like railway tracks, sigmoid and serpentine;
And soon, obedient to its destiny,
It takes its place beside the alto line.
No sooner are they joined in union
Than tenor voices with that union blend,
And as they move together on and on
A *rallentando* warns we're near the end.
Then finally, emerging from the deep,
The growling bass, our fourth participant,
Achieves that last inevitable leap
Up to the tonic from the dominant.
It is from seeing late-converging lines
We apprehend the meaning they convey,
Learning from those premonitory signs
The end is but a platform length away.
And so the music and the railway train
Roll on together merrily and thus
In single-minded harmony attain
A perfect cadence in the terminus.

HOARWITHY

Hoarwithy is a dreamy place
  Beside the River Wye.
It seems to scorn our crazy race
  As we go rushing by.
It calls to us 'Before you go
  'Another breathless mile
'Just turn aside an hour or so
  'And stay with us awhile'.

Hoarwithy seems to typify
  The Herefordshire scene.
The reddened earth is challenged by
  Its complement of green.
The fertile field, the leafy lane,
  The rolling hills express,
Whether in sunshine, wind or rain,
  Iconic Englishness.

The parish church, surprisingly,
  Fails to come up to scratch.
It's here that authenticity
  Has more than met its match.
Although it's beautiful enough,
  It's hard to reconcile
With buildings made of different stuff
  And in a different style.

The visitor may wonder what
   Its antecedents are,
But any one can see it's not
   The true vernacular.
 It's just a curiosity,
   A sight to catch the eye,
A blatant incongruity,
A statement of diversity,
An incompatibility,
A quirk of eccentricity,
A whiff of catholicity,
A gasp of incredulity,
A little bit of Italy
Beside the River Wye.

HOLE IN ONE

There is a ridge set in the Shropshire hills,
A testing-ground for any golfer's skills.
The fairway runs along the very crest,
Putting the greatest golfer to the test,
For, should he deviate to left or right,
His ball will go careering out of sight.
This skyline fairway brings him to a tee
Perched on the ridge's last extremity,
And there, a hundred feet above the pin,
That's where he senses the adrenalin.
Striking the ball with just sufficient force
To send it on its parabolic course,
A number seven iron can lift it high
Into that infinite, amorphous sky
Where it appears to hang awhile then fall,
A shining, snow-white, microscopic ball,
On to the green and purposefully roll
Into that tiny, black, inviting hole.
Such a reward is surely the supreme
Fulfilment of a golf fanatic's dream!

HOMESICKNESS

(The Roman poet, Catullus (1st Century B.C,), spent some time serving in Bithynia, (now part of North-west Turkey). In this poem he recalls how he was homesick for his father's villa on the peninsula of Sirmione in Lake Garda. The English language rarely sounds right in the twelve-syllable lines of the original Latin, so in making this translation I have used six-syllable lines alternately with ten-syllable lines. You may, if you like, think of them as representing the waves in the last line of the poem, the shorter line being the 'swash' of the breaking wave and the longer line the 'ebb' as the water drains back into the lake.)

PAENE INSULARUM, SIRMIO, (Catullus XXXI)

Half-girdled by the lake,
    Pearl among all those islands, Sirmio,
Where far-flung rollers break
    And Neptune's watery ordinances go,
How can these eyes believe,
    Which with deep longing looked for you in vain,
That I should ever leave
    Those Asian plains to visit you again?
Here let the care-worn mind
    Cast loose its burdens and be comforted;
Here, weary warrior, find
    A friendly fireside and a long-sought bed.

Let this be my reward
    For all the pain, for all the weariness:
To Sirmio restored!
    Share dearest home, your master's happiness.

Let your rejoicing soar,
    You rippling waters of the Lydian lake,
And from your deepest store,
    Wavelets, cast up sweet laughter where you break.

THE HOUSE OF MAKIN

On yonder hill the House of Makin lies,
Its roof a dome covered by ragged thatch,
Its windows, like a pair of peeping eyes,
Alert, perpetually on the watch.
Its door is standing open, and within
A row of tombstones, like a set of teeth,
Seems to present the semblance of a grin;
The doorstep's like a pouting lip beneath.
The House of Makin is a strange affair,
And when I look more closely I can see
Its curious architecture seems to bear
A striking similarity to me.
'Of course, you unimaginative ass!
'Who is it staring in the looking-glass?'

HOUSMAN AS GEOLOGIST

Had Housman understood geology
What might have happened to his poetry?

Plough straight, my lusty team, and deep,
Fear not to wake the lads that sleep
With frigid maidens, deaf and dumb,
In Onny's broad alluvium.

The lad that loved when spring began
Sleeps in the Middle Cambrian;
A fathom deep he takes his ease
And lies with *Paradoxides.*

And does my girl lie down and cry?
Nay, lad, her rosy cheeks are dry,
And other lads beside her sit
In April on the Hoar Edge Grit.

Oh, I have been to Ludlow town
And hacked the Whitcliff up and down
Extracting from the sullen stone
The steadfast and enduring bone.

The ploughman who, on Corndon Hill,
Espies the blackbird's yellow bill,
Will find no stone to curb his flight
As hard as Corndon Dolerite.

Though Shropshire yeomen rise betimes
To bear the flag to foreign climes,
I'll rest content, when battles rage,
With flags of Lower Ludlow age.

Now soon the clock will strike for me
To hang in steepled Shrewsbury
And rest my thews for evermore
In Severn's wide meander-core.

KANGAROO CHRISTMAS

Now is the summer of our discontent
Made glorious winter by this change of mood.
Out comes the tinsel and the fancy food
For lager-lubricated merriment.

On Bondi Beach it's thirty in the shade.
Celsius I mean, of course, not Fahrenheit.
Sweltering Santas make a comic sight,
Their red-nosed reindeers heading the parade.

Shepherds abiding on the Darling Downs
Watch their merinos under summer skies,
While many a doll within a manger lies
In Queensland's cities and Victoria's towns.

In Melbourne's malls and Sydney's superstores
A thin veneer of polystyrene snow
Fits curiously with the girls who go
Half naked through that oven out of doors.

How can we face the turkey, piping hot,
When all we want is half a lettuce leaf?
Our meek surrender is beyond belief;
Craven capitulation, is it not?

Just when we think there's nothing else to eat
In, like a bush-fire, comes a flaming pud!
Though it may taste exceptionally good,
It clearly must contribute to the heat.

Sydney awake! Salute the happy day!
In Martin Place a massive Christmas tree
Proclaims a summer-time nativity.
The bleak midwinter's half a world away.

Old customs honouring the birth of Christ
Were fostered in another hemisphere,
So what the blazes are they doing here?
Just bring the beer, appropriately iced!

The sound of Jingle Bells in Double Bay,
Or Good King Wenceslas on Bondi Prom
Make no more sense than that half-crazy Pom
Who breaks the ice to bathe on Christmas Day!

It makes one ask the question 'What's the point?'
While half the world dreams of a sunny clime,
The other half pretends it's winter time.
As Hamlet said, 'The time is out of joint'!

KING CANUTE

When King Canute allegedly
Sought to repulse the angry sea
His arrogant high-handedness
Was met by minimal success.
The sea, proceeding on its way,
Caused the defeated King to say
That men should not presume to do
What Nature never meant them to.
The indisputably astute
Head of the Research Institute,
Professor Pethick, PhD,
Stands on the beach at Withernsea
And, with the gift of second sight,
Declares the King had got it right;
There's simply no effective way
To hold the hungry sea at bay.
The citizens of Holderness
In inconsolable distress,
Having expended God-knows-what
Trying to do precisely that,
Now seek to stem the waves' attack
By giving Dr P the sack.
Unfortunately nobody
Has thought to tell the hungry sea,
Which still contrives to munch its way
Into the fragile boulder-clay.
In Hull the local Daily Mail
Enters this strange, contentious tale,
Urging the malcontents instead

(Exactly as the Doctor said)
To show some Yorkshire common sense
And fight for proper recompense.
Since everybody has their price,
This looks like pretty sound advice.
Meanwhile in Pethick's Institute
They're busy toasting King Canute.

LIEDER EINES FAHRENDEN GESELLEN

Between the mountains and the Baltic Sea
Stretches the land of Greater Germany,
A fertile soil which years ago had grown
Haydn and Mozart, Bach and Mendelssohn.
Musical artistry is competent
To couple scenery with sentiment,
So let's explore this varied countryside,
With Mahler as our sympathetic guide.
His lovesick youth is setting out to mend
A broken heart, with music as his friend.
Romantic music and his native tongue
Carry the footsore traveller along,
As on the heavy scented air are borne
The echoes of *Des Knaben Wunderhorn.*
The music, in its constant change of mood,
Reflects the traveller's change of attitude
As new components of the passing scene
Bring temporary joy where pain had been
And shafts of feeble sunlight fleetingly
Come breaking through the cloudy canopy.
Great swathes of forest and expansive heath
Excite the eye and take away the breath,
As comfy, cosy cottages compete
To raise a mood of pastoral retreat.
Our present landscapes are the legacies
Of evolution through the centuries;
The character of these romantic lands
Derives from nature and from human hands.
Wide flowing rivers and swift rippling rills

41

Carved passages through undulating hills
Where now a tavern's overhanging eaves
Or spreading chestnut's cupola of leaves
Proclaim a welcome in the village street
And offer shelter from the midday heat.
Earlier travellers had passed this way,
Striding along with songs of yesterday,
And as we journey through the rustic scene
We trace the self-same paths where they had been.
Where Kaspar forged his bullets in the wood
Weber contrived a hollow, echoing mood,
And as we saunter by the riverside
There in the foliage Schubert seems to hide,
Mourning his inability to win
The favours of his *Schöne Müllerin.*
The changing seasons also can reveal
Similar changes in the way we feel;
His *Winterreise* treads familiar ground
But lacks the summer's optimistic sound.
So, as the landscape and the music blend,
And, weary, we arrive at journey's end,
Mahler's unhappy hero finally
Achieves his rest beneath the linden tree.
Each country's landscape can exemplify
Music's ability to unify
The pleasures of the ear and of the eye.

A LOUSY CLASSICIST

My classroom window had a view
    Across the Shropshire Plain,
And there was I attempting to
    Employ my tiring brain,
For, as I read half-heartedly
    Those myths of yesterday
The most important part of me
    Was many miles away.

The plays of Aristophanes
    Contained a laugh or two,
But people like Demosthenes
    Just bored me through and through.
While classmates left me far behind,
    Honing linguistic skills,
My roving eye was sure to find
    Those blue remembered hills.

I wondered why they had for me
    That strong romantic pull.
I wondered why they seemed to be
    Supremely beautiful.
I wondered why Thucydides
    And all that dreary lot
Lacked the mesmeric power to please
    That Haughmond Hill had got.

That view is what I have to blame
　　For all those chances missed,
And that is why I just became
　　A lousy classicist,
And why a change of course removed
　　My worst anxiety,
And why geology has proved
　　A better bet for me.

I found out what escarpments were
　　And what the ice had done,
Came across names like Wegener,
　　Lyell and Murchison.
I scanned the county eagerly
　　And found that here and there
The Keuper Sandstone cheekily
　　Kept coming up for air.

Now that the Classics are no more
　　For me a source of dread,
I've slowly started to explore
　　What ancient poets said.
That's why you'll find me wallowing
　　In Homer's Odyssey.
Sam Butler did the decent thing -
　　Translated it for me!

MAP AND LANDSCAPE

Maps are the shorthand of geography.
They summarise a topographic tale;
They have to replicate reality,
But at a smaller, manageable scale.
So, while the roving eye can comprehend
What the immediate landscape has revealed,
Cartography permits it to extend
That comprehension to a wider field.
Imagination and the map combined,
Like any other work of graphic art,
Can reconstruct a landscape in the mind
And, through it, stir emotion in the heart.
Leave me to dream. Pass me the map again.
It is for me that peak in Darien!

MARKET STREET

Around the cosy Market place
    The red-roofed houses cling,
As children, hand-in hand, who pace
    Around a fairy ring,
Conspire to shield that hallowed space
    From every alien thing.

The men who built the stubborn town
    Upon the stubborn hill,
Their doors are fast and battened down
    Against all mortal ill.
Their beds with grass are overgrown;
    How still they lie! How still!

Today their long-forgotten foes
    Lie impotent as they.
No longer do the walls oppose
    A dangerous enemy,
Nor does an oaken gate enclose
    A strong security.

But we who in more civil days
    Have mind to pause and stare
See still the circling houses raise
    A cordon round the square,
Pierced only by the alleyways
    That enter here and there.

Whether or not some phantom feet
    Still nightly prowl about,
Treading some ghostly sentry-beat,
    I know beyond a doubt
I find a peace in Market Street
    I cannot find without.

THE MILL

A weaver lived on Calderside
   Full many a year ago.
'How hard and tedious' he cried,
   'The ways of weaving grow!
'A clattering loom
'Once shook this room
   'And it was better so.

'Beneath the hill beyond the wood
   'Where Calder bubbles by
'The conscripts of the neighbourhood
   'Their surly shuttles ply,
'And there has grown
'A trunk of stone
   'An hundred cubits high.

'O grim memorial to the old
   'And symbol of the new,
'Whereby the vendor of the gold
   'Must pay the reck'ning too!
'Sweet yesterday
'Is passed away
   'And shillings still are few.

'When Janet at her wheel was bent
     'And Mabel at her broom,
'Ere Thomas to Toronto went
     'And Terence to the tomb
'Then Eden stood
'By Copley Wood
     'And I beside my loom.'

Who Eden seeks in Sowerby
     He well may seek in vain,
But by the same accountancy
     Men ever thus complain
 In crediting
Each cherished thing
     And writing-off the pain.

MOSCHUS AT SEA

(Translated from Moschus, a Sicilian poet writing in
Greek in the Second Century B.C.)

When gentle breezes stroke the pale grey sea
My timid heart is stirred. The land no more
But the wide ocean then entices me,
But when the dangerous depths with anguish roar
And long curved waves form on the furious flood,
Then glimpsing leafy shores I flee the brine;
The land recalls me and the shady wood
And, in the rising wind, the welcoming pine.
The fisherman lives hard; a boat his home,
The sea his toil, fish his elusive prey;
But to the broad-leafed plane-tree I will come
In deepest sleep to dream the hours away.
The plaintive stream close by I love to hear,
That never tries but only charms the ear.

NATURE WATCH

Down in my garden there's a little pond
And, close beside, a cosy rustic seat.
Together with the rockery beyond
They make a sweet but absolute retreat.
There in the comfort of the evening light
I watch the antics of a little mouse,
Seeking, before the onset of the night,
The safety of her Lilliputian house.
I understand your instinct, little friend.
We too, have urges we cannot deny.
They differ strikingly, but in the end
We share that understanding, you and I.
Such was the flame, I guess, that set on fire
That troubled poet of Northamptonshire.

NORFOLK

That go from Yarmouth all the way to Lynn,
A pretty ordinary sort o' land,
A comfortable place to settle in,
To get to know, to learn to understand.

Narthin' particular to catch the eye–
The Broads, of course, they make a pretty show,
Some little hills, but never very high,
Narthin' above three hundred foot or so.

Tha's moostly farmland far as you can see,
A bit o' meadow and a lot o' plough,
Hedges and ditches, here and there a tree,
A horse or two, and here and there a cow.

But when you cross the county in the car
Through agricultural monotony,
You're suddenly surprised at where you are
In quite a different sort o' scenery.

You take the Breckland over Thetford way,
Mile after mile tha's narthin' on'y sand.
What you could do with it tha's hard to say;
Tha's just a pretty useless sort o' land.

Some hopeful farmer now and then 'll try
To grow an optimistic little crop,
A foo potatoes or a patch o'rye,
Grow it a year or two and ha' to stop.

Then years ago the woodmen come along
And make a great plantation full o' pines,
Hooge trunks o' timber, tall and straight and strong,
Like regiments drawn up in battle-lines.

Some people scorn this sort o' forestry.
They're quick enough at makin' a complaint.
They say tha's just a branch of industry;
That don't look natural. And nor that ain't.

But I don't fare to go along wi' these,
Don't judge the Breck by profitable yields;
I like to see a decent stand o' trees
Challenge the patchwork pattern o' the fields.

Then go to Swaffham or to Cockley Cley
And look at all them rows o' twisted pines,
The ghoosts o' wounded soldiers creepin' by,
Crippled an' maimed in regimental lines.

'Boo'y' for some lie mostly in the hills;
For some tha's on'y found across the sea.
Wordsworth could find it in the daffodils,
But me, I find it in variety.

A bit o' this, a little bit o' that,
Tha's what I like about the Norfolk scene.
I aren't concerned if people call it flat,
Tha's how tha' is; tha's how tha's always been.

Wrapped round the coun'y like a string o' beads
Long banks o' shingle, miles o' golden sand,
Secretive marshes thick wi' waving reeds,
Yesterday's sea, not quite tomorrow's land.

And then there's all them stately homes to see:
Sandringham, Holkham, Blickling and the rest.
Mustn't forget that parkland scenery,
Do we should more than likely miss the best.

What about Norwich then? That needle spire
Burst through the morning mist to scratch the sky.
That somehow kindle patriotic fire
And bring a tear to many a Norfolk eye.

Then all them rivers winding here and there,
Each with a separate personality,
The Bure, the Thet, the Wensum and the Yare
Hold special places in the memory.

We Norfolk folk are like a family.
Ask any Norfolk man you meet today.
Tha's ten to one he'll think the same as me.
'Norfolk?   Tha's boo'iful!'   Tha's what he'll say.

OF NAPS AND MAPS

The window in my bedroom is so maddeningly high
I cannot see a thing except the treetops and the sky.
When on a summer afternoon I take my little nap,
I lie and read the sycamore as if it were a map.

Tall branches waving in the air surmount this noble tree
Like forested peninsulas projecting in the sea,
And in the intervening space the sky is peeping through,
Injecting in the leafy green a little streak of blue.

To me this is an inlet in a littoral terrain,
A *fjord* or a *ria* in a wooded coastal plain.
I lie and watch the shipping as it passes to and fro,
Arrivals and departures as the vessels come and go.

The rules of navigation on this calm cerulean sea,
I hardly need enlighten you, are organised by me.
To navigate the channel is a tricky thing to do,
It's my imagination that will see the shipping through.

The harbour installations concentrated on the shore
Are plausibly provided by that leafy sycamore,
With pretty bays and beaches for the little kids to play
Fringing the crooked margins of that busy waterway.

This cartographic fantasy constructed in the mind
Is virtual reality of quite a special kind,
But as a helpful recipe for getting off to sleep,
The more I think about it, I'd be better counting sheep!

ON THE LINKS OF OLD ABERDEEN

Look for the loop of a seaweed-line,
  For the leathery shine
  Of marram-twine,
For the feathery, froth-blown bubble-brine
That spins from the great grey sea,
  The sea,
Forever the great grey sea.

Strain for the sound of a kittiwake's cry,
  For the screams that fly
  In the spray-grey sky,
For the sizzling, fizzling shingle-sigh
And the swash of the great grey sea,
  The sea,
Forever the great grey sea.

Feel for the crunch of the flat wet strand,
  Half sea, half land;
  With tingling hand
Feel for the sting of the wind-whipped sand
That sings to the great grey sea,
  The sea,
Forever the great grey sea.

Wait for a wave with a frightening frown
  Whose breaking crown
  Comes thundering down,
Then run for the lights of the twinkling town,
All safe from the great grey sea,
  The sea,
Forever the great grey sea!

ON THE PASSING OF AN OCCLUDED FRONT

In hospital, to make the time go by,
I watched a play unfolding in the sky,
Authored by no informed intelligence
And yet miraculously making sense.
The optimistic prologue of the play
Portrayed the onset of an April day.
Gold shafts of feeble sunlight kissed the ground,
Lighting up signs of springtime all around.
Thin mists, dissolving in the morning sun,
Shortly announced the drama had begun;
As the unclouded sun came blazing through
The sky assumed a deep cerulean blue.
On Mount Olympus pagan deities
Would plot the course of human destinies,
Inviting skilful dramatists to show
How they were implemented here below.
The present play tells how another force
Determines their inevitable course
And step by step successively presents
A pageant of predictable events.
Perceptive watchers of the sky can see
Signs of impending instability.
Thin skeins of cirrus cloud appear and trail
Like the fine fabric of a bridal veil,
Which may appear innocuous to some,
But tell a tale of turbulence to come.
The wedge-like margin of a stratus cloud,
Advancing like a white funereal shroud,
Snuffs out the twinkle of the April sun

And brings the curtain down on Chapter One.
The wind, now blowing at a faster rate,
Causes the stratus to disintegrate,
The temperature of the rising breeze
Takes a steep plunge of several degrees
As tranches of invading arctic air
Displace the warmer zephyrs everywhere.
A pall of miserable murkiness
Reduces vision to a mile or less.
Masses of crumpled cumulus arise
Into the upper reaches of the skies.
Piles of amorphous vapour wax and wane
Discharging volleys of sporadic rain.
The moody wind, now rising to a gale,
Spatters the window with a burst of hail.
The ancient deities awake and seal
Divine approval with a thunder-peal.
The interrupted visibility
Quickly returns towards infinity.
The south-west wind has now predictably
Veered to a quarter much more northerly,
Which confidently tells us that, at last,
The menacing occluded front has passed,
Conforming rigidly to Nature's plan
Just as predicted by the weatherman.
As the great playwrights of antiquity
Made story-lines conform to destiny,
The laws of science, like the gods of old,
Determine how the drama will unfold.

PICTURES IN THE FIRE

However long my life on earth may be
I don't suppose that I shall ever tire
Of one activity which pleases me,
And that is watching pictures in the fire.
Imagination underlies the game.
The cold, prosaic pyramid of coal
Bursts into life when quickened by the flame
Which gradually permeates the whole.
Pictures begin appearing here and there
As bit by bit the fire begins to glow
Until the composition everywhere
Takes on the likeness of a picture-show.
A spurt of flame uprising from the fire
Becomes a stately poplar, towering high.
Miniature clouds of silver smoke aspire
To reach a sable, soot-encrusted sky,
And as the features of the scene are changed,
And one by one the details are effaced,
The parts are gradually re-arranged
And that initial picture is replaced.
The spurt of flame that was a poplar tree
Has now become a witch's pointed hat.
We're in a witch's coven, then, and she
Emerges with her broomstick and her cat.
And as we watch those pictures in the fire
A shiny lump of coal becomes a church;
The poplar tree is now its gothic spire,
The silver smoke becomes a silver birch.
So now a cosy townscape occupies

The fireplace as the pageant marches on.
Towers of flame, striving to reach the skies,
Glow incandescent in the setting sun.
Red-glowing paths meander aimlessly
Past flanking mansions, towering left and right.
They wax and wane and vanish stealthily
Into the coal-black matrix of the night.
The black façade of still unkindled coals
Hides further secret picture-galleries
Which we can access through sporadic holes
To reach that world of fiery fantasies.
Now the proscenium that seemed to rise
Above the glossy, smooth ceramic hearth
Renounces verticality and lies
A horizontal template on the earth.
Taking advantage of this paradox
I watch from thirty thousand feet or so
Tongues of red lava gliding through the rocks,
Licking black blocks of basalt as they go.
To conjure up a realistic scene
Taxes the viewer's ingenuity.
It is a working partnership between
Inventiveness and serendipity.

RED SKY AT NIGHT

The furnaces of Frodingham outreach the sulphured smoke
That hangs about the battlefield of limonite and coke.
The fertile field that yesterday a barley harvest bore
Is ravished by a deeper plough and crops a yellow ore.

I love the fire, I love the flame, I love the crimson glow;
In them I see the likeness of the fires of long ago.
I came to love them as a child with infantile delight;
I saw them only far away and only in the night.

From Irlam burst the midnight fire that warmed my infant eye;
A surging, bloodshot fantasy, it stained the southern sky,
And often from my secret file I take a picture out
And use it for a corner-stone to build a dream about.

But now it's time for Frodingham to paint the darkness red.
Gently I wake a little boy and lift him from his bed,
And as we watch the crimson fade I wonder dreamily
If Frodingham will be to him what Irlam is to me.

THE ROAD TO NARRABRI

Among the fields of wheat that crown Australia's Great Divide
An antiquated Holden van with me and Bruce inside
Defies the unforgiving sun which burns the Aussie sky,
And hurtles menacingly down the road to Narrabri.

The Holden is protesting at the work she has to do.
She rattles like a kettle-drum and judders through and through.
We've stopped at Murrurundi for a lager and a pie,
So now it's hell for leather down the road to Narrabri.

At Gunnedah it's one o'clock. We must be there by two.
That gives us sixty minutes with a 100k to do!
We scatter all the locals in the street at Boggabri
And vanish like the clappers down the road to Narrabri.

Says Bruce 'There isn't any point in getting in a state.
'We'll call them on the mobile if we look like being late.
'She won't go any faster, though, however hard we try;
'I guess we'll have to blame it on the road to Narrabri!'

Well, here we are in Narrabri. There's nobody about.
Bruce grabs the invitation and proceeds to check it out.
He utters an expletive as he tells the reason why.
The wedding was at *twelve* o'clock - in Collarenabri!

SAINT MARY'S CHURCHYARD

Here in the heart of our community
A little haven of tranquillity
Struggles to hold modernity at bay
And keep alive a bit of yesterday.
And since the rule of nature still prevails,
The magic of this garden never fails
To generate a mood of harmony
Of peace, contentment and serenity.
Wood-pigeons fluting in the afternoon
Gently repeat their syncopated tune,
And squirrels, showing-off their expertise,
Practise their acrobatics in the trees.
A silhouette against the fading sky,
A blackbird sings an evening lullaby.
It is a recipe for happiness
When culture mingles with the wilderness.
The added bonus of a rustic seat
Contributes to the mood of this retreat,
And makes a comfortable place to sit
And think about the folk who planted it.

SCARPLANDS

On Bradlow Beacon at the break of day
One reads geology's dramatic tale,
How the keen claws of nature gouged away
The unresistant, argillaceous vale.
Alternate swathes of limestone and of shale
Like rolling breakers in a surfer's sea,
Moulding the morning landscape, never fail
To wake a sense of wonderment in me.
No human eye bore witness to the sight
When those Jurassic sediments were laid;
Only the skills of science brought to light
The processes by which these hills were made.
One reads the landscape in a different way
On Bradlow Beacon at the break of day.

SEEING AND HIDING

Give me a panoramic view
To read afresh the distant scene,
To see the hills and vales anew
And re-interpret what they mean.

But give me too the cosy glen,
The thicket and the shrubbery,
Where I can hide myself and then
Delight in my security.

So give me, best of all, a hill
Sporadically clothed with trees.
There let me lie and take my fill
Of both those opportunities.

SEPTEMBER DISTANCE, OR WEST FROM WINNIPEG

This silvered eel, nosing from east to west,
    Evokes a strange humility.
        I never guessed
The world had so much space to spend on me.

Manitoba

Eastward, where birch and shivering aspen shone,
    Beauty itself could never die,
        Now these have gone,
But distance still survives to testify.

Nature, enslaved by man, and made to fill
    Triumphant towers of blinding white,
        Works with a will
To please her lord, who cringes out of sight.

But groups of exiles, whispering in the breeze,
    Conspire to claim their lands again,,
        And shimmering trees
Creep back in clusters on the endless plain.

Saskatchewan

Although the streams below the prairie's face
   Can never see the far-away,
      They swallow space
Mile after sweeping mile to Hudson Bay.

The seasoned woods with autumn-failing leaf,
   Like Roman serfs about to die,
      In golden grief
Salute the Sun-god in the ice-blue sky.

Alberta

Now the full forest claims its rightful place.
   Alternate spires of gold and green
      Strive to efface
The wild horizons of the distant scene.

At last the crumpled crests of blue and white,
   Where the world ends in rock and snow,
      Stretch out the sight
To lengths undreamt of in the plains below.

But distance cannot die, and even they
   Taunt the imaginative mind
      And point the way
To vaster distances which lie behind.

SHOMERE POOL

Under the ceiling of a Shropshire sky,
Our senses quickened by the autumn breeze,
Sauntering through the fields my friend and I
Came to an isolated clump of trees.
October leaves still formed a canopy
Opaque enough to filter out the light,
When in that theatre of obscurity
We came upon an unexpected sight.
Right in the middle of this little wood
Appeared a hollow, weirdly wonderful;
The moss-encrusted ground on which we stood
Plunged to the margins of a stagnant pool.
In time the recollected image changed.
The tranquil pool grew rounder as it shrank.
The details of the place were re-arranged
As trees grew taller on a steeper bank.
The ink-black water, like some polished jet,
Reflected shadows of the circling wood;
A picture I was never to forget
Created an unearthly, ghostly mood.
In this re-working of the scenery
Imagination played a central role;
Enlisting fragments of reality
It brought a new *mystique* to Shomere Pool.
No gothic novel I had ever read,
No haunted house where I had ever been,
Nothing conceived in Mrs Radcliffe's head
Could match the power of that enchanted scene.
Last night a nightmare took me back again,

Stirring that adolescent memory.
I strode once more across the Shropshire Plain
Three paltry miles from steepled Shrewsbury.
Nothing could have prepared me for the crime!
The little wood that left us so amazed
Within the intervening span of time
Had systematically been erased.
Down in the bottom of the naked hole
That magic pool had turned a dirty grey.
It was as though the place had lost its soul;
All its charisma had been washed away.
Nothing our mercenary culture finds
Is proof against such philistine attacks.
Not even dreams locked up within our minds
Are safe from that annihilating axe!

A SHORT IAMBIC HISTORY OF THE ENGLISH PARK

The fashion-conscious landowner in Charles the Second's reign
Strove to impress the visitors who entered his domain
By aiming at utopia and bringing into play
Every device dictated by the fashion of the day.
Tyrannical geometry ruled in the 'pleasure-ground',
Imposing its authority on everything around.
The stamp of regularity pervaded everywhere,
Based on the perfect circle or, if not, the perfect square.
A monumental avenue now leads the curious eye
To where the park's periphery engages with the sky,
And here and there, where avenues are seen to intersect,
A column or an obelisk enhances the effect.
The ornamental water's no exception to the rule,
It must be regimented too to count as really cool.
The little ponds are circular, as round as round can be,
'Canals' are rectilinear in strict conformity.
When overcome by forces which they didn't understand
Their ancestors had deified whatever came to hand.
As death and devastation took their agonising toll
They cherished the illusion they were really in control,
And what they really wanted from their gardens, by and large,
Was re-assuring evidence that Man was still in charge.
They'd re-constructed Nature in a geometric plan
To symbolise, absurdly, her subservience to Man.
This attitude to Nature as a domineering bane
Persisted from antiquity to good King George's reign.
So, looking at the landscape from the windows of the Hall,
The Nature they encountered wasn't natural at all!
And, dispossessed of contact with their proper habitat,
The New Environmentalists began to smell a rat.
They thirsted for that ambience their ancestors had prized,

From which their own society had long been ostracised.
A growing sense of confidence encouraged them to feel
The time had come to resurrect that primitive appeal,
And, taking the savannah as the basis of the plan,
They found their inspiration in the home of ancient Man.
So, with the Hanoverians securely on the throne,
The seeds of revolution were dramatically sown.
The cultured aristocracy fanatically hailed
The diametric opposite of rules which had prevailed.
Each client sought to make his park the jewel in the crown,
Testing the capabilities of famous Mr Brown.
A crafted informality had now become the rage;
A kind of groomed savannah was the hallmark of the age.
Out of the smooth and seamless sward arose sporadic trees
Whose branches, trunks and foliage were merely there to please.
The parks were filled with ungulates to make an English 'veldt'
And every one was girdled by a dense arboreal belt.
The water-features, hitherto so rigidly confined,
Released from their restricting bonds again were free to wind.
Nature was re-instated as the undisputed queen
And freedom was in charge again where tyranny had been.
The confidence engendered by this bid to break the mould
Inspired the more adventurous to have a go for gold,
Some enterprising pioneers preferred their landscapes rough,
And thought the change of policy did not go far enough.
They viewed the new 'improvers' with unmitigated scorn,
And as the century expired the 'Picturesque' was born.
They numbered intrepidity among their greater strengths,
And carried 'back-to-nature' to unprecedented lengths.
They vilified the efforts of the Brownian Brigade,
Labelling 'bland and vapid' the improvements they had made,
And, searching for a more dramatic scenery than theirs,
Discovered in the Wilderness the answer to their prayers.

The blinding flash of sunlight and the blackness of the cave,
The thunder of the cataract, the fury of the wave,
Froze up the heart with terror as they filled the mind with awe;
Nature was in the driving-seat, and red in tooth and claw!
An enterprising owner with a promising estate
Would now review his assets in the light of the debate,
And, with a cave to hide in or a precipice to climb,
A ruin to remind him of the ravages of time,
Or just the opportunity to make a waterfall,
Even if Nature furnished him with nothing else at all,
He'd radically alter the appearance of the site
According to the principles of Messrs Price and Knight.
So what are we to think about this ever-changing tale?
To argue for consistency would be of no avail.
The legacy of pleasure-grounds which time has left behind
Are symptoms of a vacillating attitude of mind.
Successive generations of the arbiters of taste
Assented to the practices which fashion had embraced
With arrogant conviction, but pathetically soon
The pundits of posterity would come and change the tune.
More tolerant designers in the present century
Are turning back the pages of this chequered history,
And so the alternating styles of each successive age
Are lovingly enfolded in the nation's heritage.

SKY-DADOS

Just like the coloured banding on a wall
The same phenomenon can split the sky.
When sheets of leaden stratus form a pall
A streak of coloured light attracts the eye.
Between the far horizon and the cloud
Appears the sunset's golden-gleaming face,
In striking contrast with that gloomy shroud
Which bars our egress into outer space.
It's little wonder the imprisoned eye,
Trapped underneath that ceiling of despair,
Seeing that horizontal streak, will try
To reach for freedom in the evening air.
Sky-dados have a special role to play
Luring the melancholy mood away.

SNAILBEACH

A winding road ascending to the west
Surmounts the skyline of the Stiperstones
Whose quartzite outcrops punctuate its crest
Like dorsal fins or bare projecting bones.

Before descending to the River Rea
Through Myttons Beach and on to Minsterley
The road commands a prospect, far away,
Of green, quiescent English Arcady.

In that idyllic panoramic view,
Catching the magic of the evening light,
The eye's compulsively attracted to
A distant pyramid of brilliant white.

What seems to me inexplicably odd
Is that this thing I've fixed my gaze upon
Stands like the figure of some pagan god
Proudly surveying his dominion.

In fact, that patch of snow-white purity
Which forced itself on my attention so
Is nothing but the spoil of industry
Discarded by the miners long ago.

Surely, I thought, like any man of taste,
I should have been expected to resent
This brash intrusion of a heap of waste
To violate that charmed environment.

Debris, detritus, useless residue
Must surely tear the countryside apart.
How could it dare to dominate the view
While masquerading as a work of art?

Environmentalists must have their say,
Tidying up what miners leave behind.
Let them forget to clear *that* spoil away
And leave it for posterity to find.

Romantic souls who follow after us
Will see that charismatic deity
Exerting still his dominance, and thus
Preserve the myth in perpetuity.

SOLITUDE

At Morston, Blakeney, Wiveton and Cley,
Between the Norfolk farmlands and the sea,
The unfrequented coastal marshes lie,
And there a little boy of barely three,
Stunned by the sight of so much loneliness,
Fixed in his mind a picture of the place
Saving the image in his consciousness,
A horizontal sheet of empty space.
That childhood vision from the marsh's edge,
That first encounter with infinity,
That tapestry of water, sand and sedge
In eighty years has not deserted me.
The yardsticks solitude is measured by
Are Morston, Blakeney, Wiveton and Cley.

SOUTHERN UPLANDS

In summer Glasgow's populace
Comes belting to the English coast
As Scarborough is forced to face
A tartan-clad invading host.

Past Hamilton and Abington,
By Beattock and by Lockerbie,
Their every thought is focussed on
That frantic fortnight by the sea.

Inevitably on the way
They meet the English heading north
For whom a Scottish holiday
Begins beyond the River Forth,

So none of them have eyes to see
The waters of the Upper Clyde
In pastoral tranquillity
Meandering from side to side.

Were they to turn to left or right,
Seeking a perfect place to stay,
They'd find a land of pure delight
From Lammermuir to Galloway.

It's Scotland's secret beauty-spot,
Neglected by the restless hoard,
Immortalised by Walter Scott,
The doyen of the Tourist Board.

The rivers flowing to the east,
The Jed, the Ettrick and the Tweed,
Provide a veritable feast
To answer their aesthetic need.

Or if, among those rolling hills,
Their exploration westward turns,
They'd find a landscape which instils
A reverence for Robbie Burns.

But who am I to tell them what
Their preferences ought to be?
Let them dispense with Burns and Scott
And leave that paradise to me.

SUMMER MOOD

Once in the cloudbed of a summer day
I saw, or rather sensed, a little mood,
And there he played above the hollow wood
Borrowing feathers from the fluffy sky
To make an ambience, and by-and-by
Whispered a mystery and slipped away.

How many skies have stretched themselves again
To grow warm colours in the creamy light?
How many clouds as downy and as bright
Have trailed frail plumage through hot summer days,
Slowly dissolving in the heavy haze,
To tempt my little mood? But all in vain!

I learnt the other day how Dvořak sought
In foreign clouds that same elusive mood,
Chased him above some deep Bohemian wood,
And how the fugitive that sultry noon
Assumed the likeness of a haunting tune
But failed to slip his captor, and was caught.

So when I search a summer sky and see
No traces of my faithless mood at play
I'll whistle him that dreamy little lay,
Plaintively mirrored in a minor key,
Which lovers use to mourn inconstancy,
And then — who knows? — he may come back to me.

SUNSET IN THE DRAKENSBERG

(The volcanic 'Dragon Mountains' here form the
boundary between Natal, in South Africa, and
Lesotho which lies beyond the western horizon.)

In this wide world I stand,
  A wider world than what I know
    In my own land,
A world in which the darkness and the light,
Contending for possession of my sight,
  Conscript my feelings for the fight
    To gain the ground below
    And will not let me go.

Behind me in the west
  The black basaltic dragon lies
    In timeless rest.
Shieldlike he intercepts the hurtful ray
Of the stark sun, already on its way,
  That only softer shafts may play
    On this strange paradise
    Fading before my eyes.

Below me in the east
   The blackening shadows multiply.
     From the great beast
They spill like lava through the dusking plain.
Immensely distant peaks alone retain
   A pastel pink and pearly stain
     Caught from the western sky
     Until they too must die.

Slowly the daylight drains
   From vast horizons, long and low,
     Till none remains.
Only that cloud, like some huge mainsail spread
Over the sightless veldt, already dead,
   Hangs resolutely overhead,
     Still stubbornly aglow,
     The very last to go.

THE TERRACES

These are the terraces I told you of,
The quasi-foreign land of which I spoke.
The unpretentious residential row
That mimes in miniature the urban form
Becomes a stage, secluded, set apart
For local farce and native tragedy.
How coarse and angular they seem to stand,
Perched on the remnants of a cinder-bed,
These crusts of living-space! Here yesterday,
In the cold phosphorescence of the dawn
Came Jessie's babe, as one already wise.
Has he not schooled her in the baffling round
That leads from passion through the pain of love
To fear, resentment, resignation, pride
And back to love? Here come the three wise men,
Back from the nightshift with their billycans
To baby's cot and Jessie Parker's bed.
They cluck and blather at the quilted mite
And wink at Jessica as, moving on,
They go their way, unwittingly refined.
A neighbour next appears upon the stage.
See how she rides beneath full billowing sail
Of royal rags and vulgar finery!
She checks and veers, charts her uncertain course
Into the ink-black archway, and is gone,
Chased by a pang. There is a privacy
That bans the eye yet tacitly admits
One wisp of speculation to enquire
Whether she laughs or yawns or maybe weeps,

Whether she calms some doting harridan
With loving, sympathetic filial care,
Or with a blasphemy succinctly links
Her Maker with her sexuality.
Look at that animated bunch of brats!
See how they scramble up the crumbling slope
Then turn and trundle, arms and legs awhirl!
One little fellow turns his surly back
And in a world of animated dreams
Carves out great empires from the yellow waste
Of dehydrated grass. The Bridge of Sighs,
That for a visionary hour or two
Pretended to Venetian elegance,
Still catalogued in lovers' memories,
Meekly resumes its steel-and-concrete form
And spans once more a stagnant water-duct.
Our souls are vampires, thirsty parasites
That feed on the potential of the place
In which their lots are cast; and those of us
Who like to spy on other people's lives
Are given licence for a little while,
Within this most unlikely theatre
To forge a bond with those who call it home.
This is the alien land of which I spoke,
Our place of education for tonight.

THE WATER-TOWER

A late-Victorian water-tower
Exerted a mesmeric power
On my impressionable eye
Without my understanding why.
The world acknowledges at last
The merits of the recent past,
But fashion then had swept away
The favoured tastes of yesterday.
Established values fell from grace
As Modernism took their place.
Illustrious names like Mendelssohn
And Gilbert Scott and Tennyson
Were quietly disposed of in
The *cognoscenti's* rubbish-bin.
With obstinate resolve I tried
To make my way against the tide.
So in my scheme of things I prized
Items the pundits now despised.
Saint Pancras Station was for me
The peak of virtuosity,
Romantic poets still possessed
A reputation for the best.
Composers using melody
And counterpoint and harmony,
Were guarantors of excellence,
Achievers of magnificence.
So I delighted, hour by hour,
In that romantic water-tower.
The hill on which the structure stood

Was covered by a little wood
From which the building seemed to rise
Into those wide, expansive skies,
A sort of skyline sentinel
Assuring us that all was well.
A monument it seemed to be
To late-Victorian artistry,
Casting charisma far and wide
Across the rolling countryside.
The gothic pumping-house which stood
Beside it in that shady wood
Was just as fine and equally
A source of great felicity.
The tell-tale 1886,
Spelt out in decorative bricks,
Wrung from the fashion-conscious school
Derisive howls of ridicule
Which merely served to drive me on
In my perverse opinion.
Though, to be sure, I still don't know
The reason why I liked it so,
Or what was the aesthetic power
Which drew me to that water-tower,
I somehow felt myself to be
Congruous with that scenery.

THE WELSH BORDERLAND

Ghostly horizons overhang the plain
In crimpled crests of quartered meadowland,
Pricked out with sandstone and patched up with trees.
Here spreads a cosy net of little fields
Secured with hedges, wild and winterful,
Watching the year revolve. The works of man
Are mortised in the cultured wilderness.
The glum grey waters of a wintry brook,
Creeping below a lonely strand of wire,
Eat at the crumbling substance of a cliff
And trickle out of sight. The clarity
Of dead and drumming silence tunes the eye
To feel the texture of the neighbourhood
In cool defiance of a wisp of fog
That rises in the hawthorn to obscure
The inner pattern of its elegance.
Though the half-curtained sun says 'Four o'clock',
What blasphemy to measure such a scene
By the bare finger of horology,
When from the very fabric of the place
Rises the tang of the Silurian Sea!
As in the spasm of adolescent love
The being blends with an elusive prize
That tempts and taunts and seems to be attained,
So from this hill the penetrating eye
Achieves a vast communion with a sky
Grown green with age and hoary with a haze
Of figure-clouds that call the heart away.
It is as though the kernel of the soul

Were crushed and scattered on the countryside,
Infusing with its own magnetic field
The crowding, whispering hills. Hurry away
Before the cynics forge their prosy gibes
To massacre so frail a fantasy!

WEST BAY, DORSET, IN A STORM

The vapour veils are moving in as from nowhere;
　　Line upon line hurled forward they are suddenly here.

The stiff and woolly scud speeds of its own volition;
　　With measured progress it breasts the lower air.

The ashlar masonry taunts the wild waters
　　And with a low barge sends them flying.

The cold face and the smooth stone are at one in shiny wetness;
　　The land and the sea are trickling together.

The weeping of wind crowns the gruff ground of ocean;
　　The song of loneliness is set upon crunching stones.

The greenishness of grass is bleached by grey waters;
　　The colours of earth freshen without brightness.

The roofs and the houses are set apart from the sea;
　　Their population is neither numbered nor named.

The old men look out upon the empty road;
　　The old women knit and remember the fair weather.

The wildness of perception is here for the taking;
　　But there is more cheer to be had in Bridport.

WHEN GREY IS BEAUTIFUL

Unending stratus, bland and featureless,
Creates a ceiling of monotony,
Invests it with a mission to depress,
Linking the colour grey with misery.
But now the wind carves up that seamless shroud
And in a thousand vibrant shades of grey
Re-works the texture of the tattered cloud
In stark configurations far away.
Cumuloid castles hover in the skies,
Nebulous dragons posture in the air,
Counterfeit cordilleras, too, arise,
Seeking Nirvana in the stratosphere.
I can't believe that nobody but I
Can read those charcoal drawings in the sky!

WINTER SUNSET GLIMPSED THROUGH THE EDGE OF A WOOD

There is strange comfort in a darkening wood
That smells of secrets like a child's retreat.
Dimly perceived, more dimly understood,
It sets a stage where fear and safety meet.
Imagined phantoms flicker in the shade,
Sharing a refuge from the dying sky
Which, though too frail to penetrate the glade,
Holds enough heat to trap the hunter's eye.
Here some primeval man who watched the glow
Of mullioned sunsets from this hollow hide
Mastered his fieldcraft centuries ago,
Lived out his life and laid his art aside.
Can his ancestral sensitivity
To the dark wood be still alive in me?

CPSIA information can be obtained at www.ICGtesting.com
Printed in the USA
LVOW131524260812

295997LV00001B/304/P